St. Clare
(a short biography)

• • •

Joan Mueller, o.s.c.

D1456564

Franciscan
MEDIA
Cincinnati, Ohio

Cover and book design by Mark Sullivan
Cover image © iStockphoto | Robert Young

LIBRARY OF CONGRESS CATALOGING-IN-PUBLICATION DATA
Mueller, Joan, 1956-
St. Clare : (a short biography) / Joan Mueller, O.S.C.
pages cm
Includes bibliographical references.
ISBN 978-1-61636-599-8 (alk. paper)
1. Clare, of Assisi, Saint, 1194-1253. 2. Christian saints—Italy—Assisi—Biography. I. Title.
BX4700.C6M855 2013
271'.97302—dc23
[B]
2012049121
ISBN 978-1-61636-599-8

Published by Franciscan Media
28 W. Liberty St.
Cincinnati, OH 45202
www.FranciscanMedia.org

Printed in the United States of America.
Printed on acid-free paper.
13 14 15 16 17   5 4 3 2 1

Contents

Introduction

I just met a young man who named his first child "Clare." I was thrilled and wondered why he had given his little girl this name. "Because of St. Clare," he responded, eyes gleaming! I then asked him, "What do you like about St. Clare?" He immediately answered, "Because," pausing a bit awkwardly, "she followed St. Francis of Assisi."

Many Christians love St. Clare, but when pressed, they really don't know why. It is almost as though Francis, the man in love with life and nature, demands a female counterpart. Clare has always provided this harmony for Francis. Yet, when one reads the historical sources, one finds that Clare is a fascinating person in her own right, and that the primary texts regarding her life are abundant and insightful.

After the death of Francis, Roman lawyers tightened up the process of canonization. Some church prelates complained about considering Francis, this street guy with his grungy followers, a saint. Scholars at the University of Paris mocked what they considered to be Francis's flawed interpretation of Scripture. The

Franciscan brothers themselves found Francis's Rule burdensome and appealed to the papal office for various changes.

When Clare died in 1253, Pope Innocent IV, who loved her dearly, wanted to pray the Office of the Virgins rather than the Office of the Dead, effectively canonizing her immediately. Cardinal Hugolino discreetly stopped him, reminded him of the trouble this could cause, and urged him to follow canonical process. To this end, the pope ordered Bartholomew, the bishop of Spoleto, to organize a commission to examine the life and virtues of Clare according to the official process. Bartholomew did this, interviewing the sisters of Clare's Monastery of San Damiano as well as people in Assisi who had known Clare while she was at home. We still have this valuable document, known as the *Process of Canonization*, and it provides for us eyewitness testimony given under oath regarding Clare's life.

In addition to the *Process of Canonization*, we also have five writings that Clare wrote with her San Damiano sisters—Clare's *Form of Life*, and her four letters to St. Agnes of Prague. Clare's *Form of Life* outlines her monastic way of life. Her letters to Agnes of Prague provide practical and spiritual guidance and give us a glimpse into Clare's soul and prayer. These writings are invaluable reading for those who wish to understand Clare's heart and mind.

Last but not least, there is a *Life of St. Clare* written probably by Thomas of Celano, the famous biographer of St. Francis. Thomas recognized that there were details in Clare's *Process of Canonization* that needed to be clarified, and so went to Assisi to conduct further interviews with those sisters and others who had known Clare personally. There are details within Thomas's text that are found nowhere else and that do, in fact, provide information that the *Process of Canonization* does not mention.

So if your name is Clare, you love the Poor Clares, or you just wish to know more about St. Clare, this book is for you! While it is true that Clare is a faithful follower of St. Francis, she has much to say herself. Clare knew confused times, war, and poverty, and lived her life with simplicity and joy. In difficult days, she reaches across the centuries to guide us yet again.

Clare's Choice

Francis found himself fidgeting, his hands sweating a bit, as he and Brothers Philip and Bernard waited for Clare and her faithful friend, Bona, to appear. Everyone in Assisi knew about Clare's reputation for modesty and prayerfulness. The humble Brother Rufino was Clare's first cousin, and had assured Francis that Clare would certainly be open to listening to his preaching. Now, moving among the white Romanesque columns squashed into the chilly San Rufino crypt, Francis pawed his frayed robe and prayed that the Lord might open Clare's heart.

Brother Philip's eyes caught Francis's as the sound of quiet yet determined footsteps introduced the entrance of Lady Clare and her friend, Bona. Upon reaching the crypt, Clare, stunningly beautiful with heavy, long blond curls folded into a cloth veil, glanced at Francis's face and then modestly lowered her eyes. Brother

Philip offered Bona and Clare a place to sit on a stone bench, and Francis began singing what would be the theme of his preaching.

> O blessed poverty
> that provides eternal riches to those who
> love and embrace it!

> O holy poverty,
> God promises the kingdom of heaven
> and, of course,
> gives eternal glory and a happy life
> to those who possess and desire it!

> O noble poverty
> that the Lord Jesus Christ, who rules
> and is ruling heaven and earth,
> and who spoke and all things were made,
> chose to embrace before others.

Francis's eyes sparkled as his feet swayed and danced with the song. Brothers Philip and Bernard chanted repeatedly, "O holy poverty!," "O blessed poverty!," "O noble poverty!" in deep low voices accompanying Francis's evangelical cadences. Francis preached sometimes speaking in rhythm, and at other times breaking into song:

> For foxes have dens, Scripture says, and the birds of the sky have nests, but the Son of Man, who is Christ, has nowhere to lay his head. But, bowing his head, he handed over his spirit!

Francis's transition from the birds of the air to Christ's head on the cross took Clare's spirit by surprise. As if meditating upon a medieval fresco with Gospel scenes juxtaposed, Clare pondered the simultaneous mysteries of the carefree Christ playfully observing the behavior of happy-go-lucky field birds and the Christ, heart full of sorrow and body writhing in pain, on the cross. This was a glorious mediation. It held together the mysteries of Christ bound and free, suffering and joyful, human and divine.

While listening to Francis's message, Clare's soul began to imagine a life that would bring joy to her heart. She found her spirit singing with the brothers' mantra: "O holy poverty!," "O blessed poverty!," and "O noble poverty!" Francis was right, Clare recognized. Following Christ in poverty was the Gospel answer; it was the insight for which she had so long and so desperately searched.

Young Clare's world had been devastated by reoccurring violence and a lack of peace, and this lack of stability had made it difficult for her to imagine a future. Her idyllic youth was interrupted when the up-and-coming merchants and others of the town—Francis was ironically one of the merchants—went on a rampage, pillaging and burning the ostentatious palazzos of Assisi's nobility surrounding San Rufino.

Clare and her noble family escaped to the neighboring town of Perugia with their lives and remained in exile for years there with relatives. Ironically, Francis, a merchant's son, was in Perugia at this same time as a prisoner, captured by the Perugians—who sided with the Assisi nobles—after losing in a skirmish fighting over property rights and trade routes in the Assisi valley.

As a child, Clare often wondered why so many continued the quest for wealth and power. Because her family was determined to defend their wealth, they had lost their peaceful life, their freedom, and their joy. Those, like Francis, who were kept in the malarial prisons deep under the Perugian square, had gone down fighting for mercantile wealth and commerce.

Clare knew that those held in the Perugian dungeon would never return whole to Assisi. The Perugians would let them rot in the disease-infested pit until the Assisians were too ill ever to fight again. They would then dump them in the valley below Assisi so they could return as perpetual burdens to their families. Yes, Clare was very aware that wealth and power brought only misery. There was no joy on either side of the conflict.

Clare also noticed those who had no chance to be ambitious for wealth and power. Mothers with filthy, bloated children struggled daily on the Perugian streets and begged with tears and heart-breaking cries. Men who had lost their minds in the never-ending turf battles of the time sang drunken songs at night and spent their days sleeping, stinking and emaciated on the streets, slowly cooking under the Umbrian sun. Monks and nuns who had once found refuge from the world in the seclusion of their peaceful monasteries now scandalously appeared in court arguing incessantly for their financial rights. All this was the result of the greedy quest for riches.

Francis joined Brothers Philip and Bernard in their mantra for a time and then continued preaching:

Certainly you know that the great Lord when coming into the virgin's womb chose to appear contemptible, needy, and poor in this world. He did this so that human beings, who were utterly poor and needy, suffering from a dire lack of heavenly food, might be made rich in him in the kingdom of heaven that they will certainly possess. So, exalt exceedingly and rejoice, filled with great joy and spiritual happiness.

Oh, happiness, Clare thought! Had she ever heard anyone speak of happiness? As she shivered both from the dampness of her stone bench and from her excitement over Francis's message, Clare's mind settled on her perpetual worry: her Uncle Monaldo's plot to marry her to Lord Ranieri. Not that Lord Ranieri was the worst possible choice, but the thought of being sucked into a nobleman's insatiable appetite for wealth and land while engaging in murder, rape, and plunder to seal his perceived rights overwhelmed and sickened Clare. She wanted to be with the Lord and enjoy God's peace. There was no peace in the pursuit of riches: she knew this in her very core.

"O holy poverty!" "O blessed poverty!" "O noble poverty!" Brothers Philip and Bernard chanted. Clare closed her eyes and felt herself transported into peace. She could hear her companion, Lady Bona, humming softly with the brothers' mantra as Francis preached.

> If contempt of the world pleases you more than honors,
> poverty more than temporal riches
> and storing up treasure in heaven rather than on earth,
> then you will be rewarded in heaven.
> For heaven's treasure is not consumed by rust, destroyed by moths,
>   by moths,
> or stolen by thieves.
> And you will quite fittingly be called sister, spouse, and mother
> of the Son of the Most High Father and the glorious virgin.

"Yes," Clare's heart exclaimed. She had thought about entering religious life before, but the wealth and power of the monasteries outlining the Assisi countryside did not inspire her. The established monasteries had many possessions, vast tracts of land, and numerous serfs. Some retained armed knights who were quite willing to cut down anyone who trespassed or stole from the monastic reserves. Clare's mother had educated her daughter well, and Clare feared that she might even end up leading such a community, worrying day and night about its finances and, God forbid, finding herself in court arguing to protect its wealth.

There were also small beguine-like monasteries dotting the hills and valleys surrounding Assisi. The women who lived in these convents worked to provide for their needs, but their place in the church was ill-defined and their way of life revolved around the work of their inhabitants. These sisters did not want to marry, and lived together in community finding in each other a degree of safety and financial interdependence. Clare admired their courage and ingenuity, but wanted a religious lifestyle that would focus, not so much on making a living, but on prayer and devotion.

Now, as she listened to Francis, she began to envision her own path. She would live a monastic life like the Benedictines she knew well, but within her enclosure she would be content to live in poverty. Instead of wanting more and more, she would be happy with little. She would store up treasure in heaven rather than on earth.

Marrying the Poor Christ

A cool March breeze brushed Clare's face as she realized she had escaped. She did not notice that her beautiful white dress was soiled from her flight through the cellar of the Offreduccio house. She had escaped through the "door of death," a back door meant to offer a getaway to those living in the Offreduccio household if the front of their grand palazzo was attacked.

As Clare descended from Assisi, her heart raced with excitement. The Lord had shown her the way; her life's journey had begun. It was Palm Sunday evening. That morning she had gone to church with her mother and sisters and entered into the mystery of the Lord's passion. The Lord came into Jerusalem and the people waved palm branches to welcome him. His journey from death into life had begun. Clare was entering this journey with her beloved Lord. She had passed through the door of death and was entering a new life.

Guido, the bishop of Assisi, had been kept well-informed concerning Clare's choice. He had certainly not agreed to it easily. Francis and his brothers had returned not long ago from Rome and had received papal permission to preach repentance to all. Guido knew that he could call on the brothers anytime and that they would do work in the diocese that needed to be done—nurse lepers, clean churches, patch ceilings, and so on.

Clare's choice, however, was different. Not that he was opposed to Clare giving her dowry to the poor—this would take the powerful Offreduccio family down a notch, something attractive to the bishop, who was one of Assisi's most powerful landowners in his own right. Perhaps it was Clare's beauty, or maybe it was her innocent piety that Guido felt so enticing. He was a churchman, but Clare had true belief. When she approached Guido to receive the Eucharist, Guido saw in her a faith unlike any other. He envied that faith.

The pious Clare, however, was no pushover. When she revealed to the bishop her thoughts of being married to Christ, Guido encouraged her to enter the powerful Benedictines at the Monastery of San Paolo. There she would join other noble women in a life of prayer and devotion, and her future would be financially secure. Clare, however, wanted to follow the Poor Christ as Francis and his brothers were doing, not by preaching in public but by living within a monastery protected by faith in Christ alone.

Guido never would have approved of the plan, but when Clare presented him with the alternative, he found that he did not have a counter argument. If Clare did not do as she proposed, she would be compelled to marry into the world of despair, violence, rape, and greed that was eating the very soul of Assisi. Even the successful Guido understood that his vast tracts of land along with his power and influence did not bring him happiness. He was struck by the young Clare; he did not want to destroy the radiant beauty of her soul, and in the end, he found himself giving in to her wishes.

As Clare breathlessly entered the valley, she could see torches flaming in the distance. The song of friars filled the moonlit evening, and she could pick out the voices of Brothers Philip and Bernard chanting: "O holy poverty!" "O blessed poverty!" "O noble poverty!" Surrounding Clare, the brothers escorted her to the tiny church of St. Mary of the Angels. There Francis greeted her with a welcome and a blessing of peace.

Entering the church, Francis moved toward the altar with Clare, and the brothers crammed into their places. The light from the torches flickered on the gray stone walls, and Clare could not imagine a more beautiful sight. She glanced down and noticed that the bottom of her dress was muddied and smudged, but even this gave her only joy. She was choosing the path for her life. She was about to marry the Poor Christ and live with him forever.

Kneeling before Francis with the brothers continuing their chant, Clare lifted her veil bit by bit as Francis cut her thick blond curls. Francis then placed a large sack over Clare's head, and turned to unite the friars in prayer while Clare discreetly removed her white dress, tied the sack to her small waist, refastened the veil to her shaven head, and rejoined Francis. Francis smiled at the radiance of the woman who stood beside him. Some of the brothers openly wept, while others sang with more gusto. Gathering around Clare, they moved out of the chapel and into the oak grove outside. There each brother greeted their new sister, and congratulated her as she stood next to Brother Francis.

The midnight hour approaching, Francis with Philip, Bernard, and Clare began the short journey to the Benedictine Monastery of San Paolo. This established and well-endowed monastery had the advantage of a papal protection that automatically excommunicated those who had the audacity to attack any woman who took refuge within its walls. Bishop Guido, convinced of Clare's resolve, had arranged with the monastic abbess for Clare's protection. The brothers now accompanied Clare to this monastery where the guards, waiting for their arrival, welcomed them and permitted Clare to enter.

Settled within the monastic quarters, Clare rested on her bed in silence. Her heart was ecstatic, as she had found her one desire. Her fingers reached toward her shaven head as if still unconvinced that the deed had been done. No longer was she marriageable looking like this. No man would accept her dowry now. She was free, free to follow her Lord.

chapter three

Disowned

Lady Ortolana wondered why Clare had not appeared early Monday morning of Holy Week. Searching for her within the women's quarters of the large Offreduccio palazzo, she realized with horror that her daughter was nowhere to be found. She inquired whether she was perhaps with the neighbors, but no one had seen her. She approached the night watchman, John de Ventura, who insisted that Clare had to be somewhere within the house and joined the frantic search.

Moving into the cellar, John discovered that the beam barring the back door was unbolted. Calling to Lady Ortolana, he related the news but had no explanation for the misplaced latch. Could Clare have lifted the heavy beam by herself? There was no one who had entered to help her—the watchman was certain of this, since Palm Sunday evening was quiet. No one had arrived or left by the front door of the house.

With all possibilities exhausted, Ortolana approached Monaldo, the family patriarch, with the upsetting news. Monaldo confronted John, the night watchman, who assured him that no one had entered or left the house by the front entrance the evening before. However, the watchman admitted, the back door was unlatched. Perhaps Clare left the palazzo in this way, although he doubted that Clare could have lifted the heavy beam by herself.

Monaldo was puzzled, but there had to be an obvious explanation. Clare was no vagabond. She had always stayed within the enclosure of the house unless accompanied by other young women of the aristocratic San Rufino square. Having again searched every corner of the house, Monaldo sauntered into the square—trying to make light of the fact that an Offreduccio woman in his charge was indeed nowhere to be found—and inquired whether Clare was in this house or that. He tried to keep his cool, exhibiting knightly honor despite the fact that it increasingly appeared that he had been duped by an unmarried woman in his own household!

The gossips, of course, took enormous delight in Monaldo's predicament and inquired here and there with feigned anxiety as to Clare's whereabouts. After a few hours, a report from the valley reached the San Rufino plaza. Clare, according to the rumormongers, had taken refuge in the Monastery of San Paolo.

Taken completely by surprise, Monaldo had difficulty hiding his rage, although he publically laughed off the tittle-tattle. He could feel his gut churn as his suspicions mounted. He knew the bishop, a rival landowner, was not above subverting the business interests of the Offreduccio family. If Clare became a Benedictine nun, all arrangements for marrying her into the wealth of Lord Ranieri's family would be moot. Yes, Monaldo admitted inwardly, the bishop is responsible for this insolence, but he would go into the valley and return Clare, as well as recover his family's honor. He would not be trounced by the vile schemes of an avaricious churchman.

Storming back to the palazzo and ignoring the watchman's continued insistence that nothing the night before had seemed out of the ordinary, Monaldo shrieked his summons to the other Offreduccio knights. Those within earshot immediately mounted their horses and rode off to gather relatives. Lady Ortolana shuddered. While Clare's disappearance did take her by surprise, she knew that her daughter did not desire marriage.

Clare had always listened attentively to the scriptures, learned her Latin eagerly, read the psalms prayerfully, and treasured the stories of women martyrs who gave their hearts to Christ alone. Yet, Ortolana couldn't quite imagine Clare being happy with the Benedictines. The San Paolo nuns, while well-established, wealthy, and powerful, seemed more preoccupied with retaining their earthly wealth than with loving God with all their hearts. Would her daughter be happy with them? Certainly time would tell.

While Ortolana pondered the mystery of her daughter's choice, Monaldo and six other Offreduccio knights rode with fury to the Monastery of San Paolo. The dust from the horses blanketed the steep Assisi slope and a black cloud followed them as they rode hard through the valley. Monaldo was not going to let a lucrative marriage contract slip through his fingers. Clare would return with them. He would make sure of this!

Approaching the monastic gate of San Paolo, Monaldo's demeanor abruptly changed. Over time the abbesses of San Paolo had negotiated papal privileges for their monastery. They were exempt from civil taxes and church tithes. In times of interdict, the sisters were able to continue to hear Mass and pray their Office. A woman who sought entrance into the San Paolo monastery was protected from familial interference. Any relative who tried to molest her or impede her right to enter the monastery could be excommunicated.

After the monastic guards had gathered the Offreduccio swords at the entrance, a small nun escorted Monaldo and his cohorts into a parlor where they waited for the abbess to make time for them. Confronted with monastic silence, the need to hush their voices initially calmed their rushing adrenaline, but the waiting gradually riled further Monaldo's indignation. When the abbess and her vicaress finally appeared, they offered the men refreshments and a blessing, reminding them that they were in a religious household.

During the conversation that followed, the abbess informed the knights that Clare was not, in fact, seeking entrance into the Benedictine monastery. One can imagine the relief Monaldo felt when hearing this news, only to learn in horror that Clare was intending to join Francis and his ragtag group of brothers. This was an upset that Monaldo's thin-shelled civility could not withstand. He demanded to see Clare in order to return her to Assisi. With this, the abbess and her vicaress excused themselves, offering time again for the impetuous Monaldo to cool his heels.

Meanwhile, in the monastic church, Clare prayed before the Blessed Sacrament begging for protection and grace for the confrontation she knew was coming. Feeling a light tap on her shoulder, she turned to see the kind face of the abbess who had so graciously agreed to protect her. "Your uncle Monaldo is looking for you," Clare was informed. Clare knew she was protected within the monastic walls, and yet her heart still skipped a beat. "Stay here," the abbess whispered quietly. "I will bring them to you."

Clare listened to the approaching footsteps as she made her way steadfastly to the altar. Grabbing hold of the altar cloth, and determined not to be separated from her Lord, Clare begged for grace and mercy. Within her heart, a voice assured her, "I will always protect you." Smiling at the tender consolation, the young bride prepared to stand her ground.

Upon spotting Clare, Monaldo pushed past the abbess and her vicaress and shoved his way toward the altar as if sprung from a cage. Forsaking every ounce of Christian upbringing, he yelled at the top of his voice as the abbess and her vicaress forcefully hushed him. Looking her uncle squarely in the eyes, Clare held on to the altar cloth with one hand and with the other removed the veil covering her sheared head.

Monaldo stopped dead in his tracks, audibly gasping in horror. The lovely Clare, who he had thought would bring his family wealth and a powerful alliance, was a mutilated wreck. No one would marry her now. She had ruined herself, and for what? To be a nun in a reputable monastery? No! She—a woman—intended to follow Francis of Assisi! Monaldo couldn't comprehend such an outrageous plot. His face scarlet with fury, he screamed at the top of his lungs not even registering that the abbess and vicaress were there as witnesses, "You are no longer an Offreduccio, Clare! You are disowned! You are disowned!"

Storming out of the church, Monaldo led the Offreduccio knights past the abbess and her vicaress, and reclaimed their armor at the gate. As they mounted their horses, Monaldo was tempted to pay Francis a visit. The other knights, however, knew that beating up defenseless churchmen who were nursing lepers would only bring further contempt upon the family. "Let her go," they cautioned. "She is useless now. She is gone. She is lost. She is dead to us."

Alone at the altar, Clare nearly collapsed from terror and relief. She knew that Monaldo had no compunction when it came to beating a woman. She was happy to have escaped with her life and limbs intact. She was free. She was disowned before witnesses. She could now live without fear.

chapter four

Catherine's Ordeal

The next morning, the abbess at San Paolo sent a messenger to the brothers staying at St. Mary of the Angels. "Clare's family has publically disowned her. There is no further need for Clare to remain in the protection of this monastery." Upon receiving the welcomed news, Francis immediately fell on his knees thanking God for such kindness and mercy. He was glad that the Offreduccio knights had decided to return directly to Assisi rather than to come to St. Mary of the Angels to take their revenge. Clare was now totally free to follow the Poor Christ. She could fulfill her heart's desire. The message of the Gospel had inflamed her soul, and she could love the Lord in freedom and peace.

Francis and his brothers were rebuilding the rundown house once used by old Father Pietro who had been the resident priest at the little church of San Damiano. San Damiano was the first church that Francis had restored after his conversion to the Lord.

It was in this little church that Francis took refuge praying before its icon of the Lord on the cross, asking that Christ might show him the path for his life. With even a recollection of this holy image, Francis silently mouthed the prayer that he had repeated so often when he was desperately seeking God's desire for his life.

> Most high, glorious God,
> Illumine the darkness of my heart.
> Give me an orthodox faith,
> persevering hope,
> and perfect charity.
> Lord, give me sense and knowledge
> so that I will always do
> your holy and true command.

Even in these early years, Francis dreamed of women who would spend their lives following the Poor Christ and praying for his brothers and the world. He had heard of Clare's reputation for holiness, and wondered if she might lead local women who would desire such a life. Now, Clare had been disowned and was free to move forward.

Thankfully one of the brothers had a relative who lived with the beguine-like sisters in the convent of Sant'Angelo just up the hill a bit from San Damiano. The sisters there had assured him that Clare would be welcome. Even if the house attached to the San Damiano church was finished, Clare would first need companions to stay with her. But who would join Clare in such a radical choice?

Settling in with the Sant'Angelo sisters, Clare immediately began working for her keep and praying for a companion. She had shared with her younger sister, Catherine, the preaching of Francis and hoped that perhaps Catherine would find a way to join her. Her good friend, Lady Bona, was now back from a pilgrimage to Rome but Clare knew that a poor, religious lifestyle would not be her choice. As the days passed, Clare begged God to give her a companion. She pleaded with God to open Catherine's heart.

Clare did not have to pray long. Within a few weeks, Catherine appeared at the Sant'Angelo monastery eager to join her sister. When news reached the Offreduccio household that Catherine was with Clare at Sant'Angelo, the infuriated Monaldo gathered twelve knights and raced to the monastery. This small church, he knew, was unguarded. Clare, he would leave there—she deserved such a fate, since her shorn head made her useless—but Catherine, he would return. He would not lose two Offreduccio women to a dim-witted, half-baked scheme! Clare had not even had the decency to remain with the Benedictines, but instead involved herself with the merchant's son—Francis Bernardone—a no-good, religious fanatic whose ambitions to preach were somehow blessed by both the bishop of Assisi and by the pope himself! Monaldo would have no more of this! Catherine would return.

The pounding of horses' hooves announced the trouble. Pushing aside the sister at the gate, the Offreduccio knights, Monaldo in front, entered the church of Sant'Angelo contemptuous of both the silence appropriate to the place and the dignity of their class. Screaming obscenities, and finding Clare and Catherine in the church, Monaldo slammed Clare to the ground and grabbed Catherine by the wrist.

Catherine shrieked in pain, but managed to wriggle out of Monaldo's grasp before realizing that Monaldo also had her caught firmly by the hair. "Let me go," Catherine screamed, but

Monaldo, profanities in plenty, grabbed her waist in an attempt to subdue her. "Let me go," Catherine cried again, "Clare, help me, do not let me be taken from Christ our Lord!"

Clare still reeling from her blow, ran after her sister only to again be hurled to the floor and stamped on by one of Monaldo's thugs. Others of the Offreduccio company, however, were visibly stunned by Monaldo's behavior. Abusing Offreduccio women this cruelly in public and, even more despicably, in a church, was unchivalrous behavior. Clare was now a woman of the church and attacking her was a dishonor that they did not want attached to their name. The sisters of Sant'Angelo were witnessing the event and had relatives in Assisi and Perugia. The news of Monaldo's sacrilegious brutality would soon be public.

Stepping into the fray, the knights, Hugolino and Scipione, attempted to shield Catherine from Monaldo's fury. "Let her be," Hugolino glared into Monaldo's eyes. But Hugolino's interference further infuriated Monaldo as he carried Catherine outside. Obstinate, he twisted Catherine's hair around his fist, grabbed his horse by the reins, and dragged her across the small Sant'Angelo courtyard. "You will come with us," he howled, "if I have to drag you by the tail this horse." He slapped the back end of his mount just as they began making their way up the path to Assisi. The horse bolted, and Monaldo, reaching to bring it under control, pulled out a clump of Catherine's hair at the roots. Catherine screamed in anguish, but the livid Monaldo was past compassion. He would not be outdone by another Offreduccio woman. He was the patriarch of the family. He would be obeyed.

Meanwhile, Hugolino again attempted to talk Monaldo down. "We can't take her back to Assisi like this!" he pleaded. "Please, Monaldo, listen." Hugolino looked with horror at Catherine's face, bruised and swollen. Her head was bleeding profusely and her lovely hair was matted with thickening blood and dirt. Just then, her body suddenly went limp. Was she still alive? There was so much blood! What had Monaldo done? Would Catherine ever recover? Better to leave her with Clare than to enter the cathedral square with an Offreduccio woman beaten by her own protector!

Scipione sided with Hugolino. "Monaldo," he ordered. "Let go of her!" "We need to get out of here." "She is dead. Let her alone." Monaldo gave Catherine one last merciless kick. She squealed in pain, revealing that she was not yet dead. Lifting his hand, Monaldo aimed for her skull ready to finish the job. At this, both Hugolino and Scipione bolted, held him back, and forcefully walked him forward. "Leave her here, Monaldo," Scipione ordered. "She is dead to us. She is nothing. She is of no use to us now." Monaldo held his chest as though he were in grave pain. Face scarlet with fury, he tore his arms away from Hugolino and Scipione. The other knights circled him preventing him from turning back. They would leave the young woman in the dirt. She was dead to them.

As the knights ushered Monaldo up the path toward Assisi, a few of the sisters at Sant'Angelo helped the wounded Clare search for her sister. When Clare spotted Catherine lying motionless on the path, she ran forward hoping against hope that her sister was alive. As she approached, she gasped at her bloodied head and broken body. Clare howled and collapsed over the seemingly lifeless body when Catherine suddenly coughed and looked at her with pained eyes and a faint smile. Ecstatic, Clare shouted to the other sisters who ran back to the monastery to find a cloth by which they could carry Catherine to Sant'Angelo.

As the days passed, Clare nursed her bruised and battered sister. She gently washed her wounds and fed her vegetable broth and soft foods. The warm spring mountain air and lighthearted songbirds seemed to encourage her recovery, and within a few weeks, she was feeling better although still bearing telltale signs of her ordeal.

chapter five

San Damiano

While Catherine recovered, Francis and his brothers worked tirelessly to ready the small house connected to the San Damiano church. When the day arrived for Clare and Catherine to move in, the brothers gathered, and Clare, with head covered, and Catherine, with hair long and flowing except for the obvious patches that had been viciously pulled out by her uncle, knelt before Francis and promised him obedience.

Seeing Catherine's still-oozing scabs, Francis fought back his emotion and then inquired: "What do you ask God?" Francis's voice always rang rich and true, but the sight of Catherine's injuries choked him. Moved with compassion toward this slight young woman and the strength of her caring sister, Francis realized that their love for the Poor Christ was real. These women were not infected with a fleeting religious enthusiasm. Clare and Catherine were true sisters to Francis and his brothers. They did not fear poverty, labor, trial, disregard, and the contempt of the world. In Catherine's still weak but genuine smile, Francis even discerned that she bore her wounds with delight as she won them in imitation of the Poor Christ whom she loved.

Taking his shears gently to Catherine's hair, Francis began the hymn to holy poverty while Clare and the brothers sang along. He then drew from his sleeve a small piece of parchment and read:

> Because by divine inspiration, you have made yourselves daughters and handmaids of the Most High King, the Father of the heavens, and have espoused yourselves to the Holy Spirit, choosing to live according to the perfection of the holy Gospel, I resolve and promise for myself and my brothers always to have the same attentive care and special solicitude for you as for them.

Francis gave the parchment containing these words to Clare who kissed it and fought back her tears. He then addressed Catherine: "You have suffered like the virgin martyr, Agnes of Rome. In her honor and in memory of your courage, you will be called Agnes."

Both Catherine and Clare beamed at Francis's insight. Their mother, Ortolana, had often told them the story of Agnes of

Rome, who had been murdered in her determination to follow Christ. Having Catherine carry the living memory of this most glorious woman martyr into the San Damiano monastery was a joy beyond belief. Catherine had indeed suffered, but her agony seemed as nothing compared to her joy.

In the quiet of their new home, Clare and Agnes prayed as nuns and lived as paupers. From Clare's perspective, this was as close as heaven could be to earth. Joining the angels in heaven with their songs of praise, the sisters cared little for the things of earth. No one was jealous of their small church and house. Theirs was a quiet life, a life of peace, a life of prayer.

Soon other women began to understand the wisdom of Clare's insight. While religious who fought in courts over their rights regarding land and serfs were common fodder for neighborhood gossips, Clare and Agnes lived peacefully, protecting nothing. They planted a small garden and lived on the donations given them by pious visitors. Brothers returning from their daily labors or who had begged for them brought them bread and oil and asked for prayers. Friends from Assisi and Perugia made sure that they had the basic necessities of life.

As time passed, other women came to San Damiano wanting to join Clare and her sister. Among Clare and Agnes's first companions were Pacifica; Benvenuta; Benedetta; Cristiana; Agnes, daughter of the lord who would become the mayor of Assisi; Balvina; Francesca; and others. As these women joined, they had to decide how to pray, live, eat, and form a community marked by work, prayer, and poverty. They were distinguished from other local monasteries of women because they did not have stores of money, valuable gems, silver or gold, luxury items, or real estate with rights to serfs, bridges, water, or mills. They were not litigious, they did not argue with the bishop over tithes, and they were not demanding money as rents.

Rather than join the wealthy to the detriment of the poor, income that came to the sisters was given to the poor for their relief. Throughout her life, Clare desired to live the words of the holy Gospel: "If you wish to be perfect, go, sell your possessions, and give the money to the poor, and you will have treasure in heaven; then come, follow me" (Matthew 19:21).

The Privilege of Poverty

Today, the monasteries of Clare's sisters are described by what Clare referred to as "the one thing necessary": her love affair with the Poor Christ, and the nuns are known as "Poor Clares." Clare understood that God became poor for our sake so that our very humanity might be transformed. Christ became poor so that we might become sons and daughters of God. Or, as the early Church fathers used to say, "God became human, so that human beings could become divine."

When Francis began his order, he had one entrance requirement. If a brother wanted to enter into a life of penance, he was to follow the Gospel and sell everything he had and give it to the poor. When Clare decided to follow Francis, she did the same thing. She sold her inheritance and gave it to the poor. While other nuns and monks gave their dowries to their monasteries, Franciscans lived without the regular income from endowments. Rather than giving of their surplus to the poor, Franciscans gave all they had to the poor and then remained content to live with the poor in their circumstances.

Monks and nuns who lived in monasteries accepted individual poverty—meaning that they did not personally own property, real estate, or luxury goods. This is still the type of poverty most religious orders profess today, and it is the poverty recognized in canon law. What Francis and Clare envisioned, however, was a different type of poverty.

While feudal lords controlled old wealth, and while the merchant classes were able to invest in luxury products coming from the East, the poor found themselves with virtually nothing. They did not own property, they were often homeless, they were sick without access to medical care, and they were hungry. While small villages often helped those in their midst who found themselves in dire straits, those preoccupied with wealth in the growing medieval towns and cities felt less immediate compunction to respond to the needs of their neighbors.

When they turned to the church, the poor encountered monasteries that supported themselves through land rights, rents, water rights, road tolls, timber rights, and other means. The poor were often obligated to pay rents, taxes, and tolls to these monasteries. For the destitute, a monastery might give alms, but these alms were often paltry compared to the rents and tithes the poor owed monks and nuns. As a result, monasteries were often seen as just another manifestation of the feudal economy that whittled the poor out of their ability to earn a sufficient living.

In the twelfth and thirteenth centuries, new orders who professed not only individual poverty but also communal poverty, who did not own real estate or property, and who gave their riches away to the poor were seen by many as following Christ more perfectly.

While wandering preachers such as Francis and his brothers might support themselves with day work and occasional begging, Clare and her sisters lived an enclosed life as religious women in the Monastery of San Damiano. The papacy in the thirteenth century did not want wandering and begging nuns, and Clare and her sisters not only accepted enclosure but embraced it. Their lives were spent in prayer and in the work necessary to their common life. Unlike other monasteries, the sisters did not have servants to clean, wash clothes, and do other menial labor. They spent their days doing these tasks themselves.

San Damiano was located on the mountainside just outside of Assisi, and it was surrounded by the rural poor who lived around the monastery and in the valley. These people often came to San Damiano with small gifts for the sisters—some oil, perhaps, some bread, or some wood. In return they would tell the sisters their problems and the sisters would promise their prayers.

In one case, a little boy pushed a pebble up his nose and his parents were unable to dislodge it. They rushed the child to the monastery and begged to see Clare. Praying over the child—and in the process calming everyone's nerves—the pebble dropped from the child's nose and all was well again. This is a simple story, but it shows that the people around Clare's monastery were ordinary people with ordinary family problems. Clare's sisters lived in their midst. They were engaged in their lives and were grateful for the small gifts the poor gave to them.

When the peasants came to San Damiano with their simple gifts, Clare and her sisters were deeply thankful for them. They did, in fact, truly need these donations. Because the sisters were grateful for gifts given, responded to the real problems of ordinary people, and prayed for their needs, those living around the San Damiano monastery loved Clare and her sisters.

When Clare speaks of her love for the Poor Christ, she is not referring to an abstract mysticism. She knows and sees the Poor Christ in her sisters, in her neighbors, and in the poor who depended on the monastery for their spiritual and moral support. Yet, poverty, for Clare, was not a mere social program. When Francis preached to her, he preached in the words of the Gospel: "If you wish to be perfect, go, sell your possessions, and give the money to the poor, and you will have treasure in heaven; then come, follow me" (Matthew 19:21).

Religious life, often called "the life of perfection," was the response to Christ's call of the young man who wanted to do something more for God. If you wish to lead a religious life, according to the Gospel, you need to sell what you have and give it to the poor. It was a simple program, and Clare and Francis wanted to follow the Gospel literally.

Love of the Poor Christ was the very foundation of Clare's vocation. She often meditated on the Christ who came into this world as a poor baby, wrapped in swaddling clothes and laid in a manger because there was no room for him in the inn. Clare wondered at the marvel of God becoming human. Not only had God become human, but he chose to be born among the poor, in poor conditions. Mary and Joseph were not even at home for his birth!

Clare also pondered the public life of our Lord. Jesus wandered the earth without a place to lay his head. When he preached, he depended upon the generosity of others for his food and shelter. He worked with his disciples, catching fish in order to provide an evening meal. The ministry of Christ was not financially endowed. Rather, the Lord depended upon the mercy of God for his day-to-day living.

Most marvelous for Clare was the consideration of the passion of Christ. Christ was considered by the religious men of his day to be a nobody—to be held in low esteem. Among contemporaries, there were few who were merciful toward him. He was held in contempt, spit upon, battered, and scorned. He took upon himself our sins, so that we might be washed clean in his blood. Clare pondered wound after wound of our Lord, weeping over the depths of his passion and pain.

In all this, certainly she also held in her heart the pain of many who came to the monastery—a child with cancer, a dying mother, a mentally ill son. She united in her prayer the sufferings of her neighbors to the sufferings of Christ. Christ did not run away when he experienced the depths of human poverty and misery. The Poor Christ became one of us, stayed with us, and raised us up.

Clare was in love with this Poor Christ. Her dedication to poverty permitted her to stay with her beloved Christ, to suffer what he suffered, to delight in his delights, and to accompany those who suffer misery into resurrected hope.

While Clare's life was permeated with joyful prayer and discerning care of her sisters, there was one thing that she would not compromise. She had founded the San Damiano monastery as a home for those who wished to follow the Poor Christ according to the words of the holy Gospel. This poverty was, for Clare, both her identify and treasure.

An Ordinary Life

As noted in the Introduction to this book, after Clare's death, Pope Innocent IV commissioned Bishop Bartholomew of Spoleto to place witnesses to Clare's life under oath and to gather from them information regarding Clare's holiness. From this legal proceeding, we possess Clare's *Process of Canonization*. In this *Process*, the sisters who lived with Clare tell us how Clare lived her life in the San Damiano monastery.

From Sister Pacifica we learn that Clare spent her nights prostrated in prayer. She often prayed Francis's *Office of the Cross* and the *Prayer of the Five Wounds of the Lord*. Keeping the passion of Christ always in her mind, she wore a small cord with thirteen knots under her habit as a reminder of the Lord's wounds and she often prayed with tears in her remembrance of Christ's passion.

At midnight, Clare would light the church lamps and ring the bell for Matins. If the sisters slept through the bell, she would gently wake them for prayer. Clare often received the sacrament of confession, and was so aware of Christ's presence within the Holy Eucharist that she visibly trembled when receiving Communion. She would often say: "God has given me a gift today that heaven and earth cannot contain!"

In her interview, Sister Pacifica revealed that she had been Clare's neighbor in the San Rufino piazza and had joined Clare at San Damiano as one of her first companions. She told a delightful story of Brother Bentevenga, a Franciscan brother who used to beg for the San Damiano sisters.

During the second year that they were at San Damiano, the sisters did not have oil for their lamps, so Clare asked Brother Bentevenga to go out and beg some for the sisters. Clare washed a container and placed it near the entrance of the house so that Brother Bentevenga could use it when begging. About an hour later, when Bentevenga came looking for the container, he found it filled with oil. He searched the area trying to determine who had filled it, but no one claimed responsibility. The sisters never did discover who had given them the oil. In one sense, it didn't matter. Clare and her sisters needed the oil, and God found a way to provide it for them.

In other accounts, we learn that while the fruits of Clare's prayer encouraged and consoled the sisters, her penance and abstinence caused them concern. Clare was so strict with her fasting that the sisters could not understand how she survived. On Mondays, Wednesdays, and Fridays, she ate nothing at all, and on other days she had only bread and water. Of course, this regimen eventually undermined her health. Both Francis and the bishop of Assisi stepped in and ordered her to eat at least a half a roll of bread during her Monday, Wednesday, and Friday fasts. On Sunday, Clare drank a bit of wine when it was available.

Clare also maintained the strictest poverty in regard to her clothing. She had only one tunic made of the poor, rough wool worn by peasants. If she noticed that a sister's tunic was more tattered than hers, she exchanged her clothes with that sister. As a penance, she wore a boar's hide or horsehair shirt under her tunic with the bristles on her skin. When Clare became ill, the sisters took these shirts away from her.

While Clare's medieval penances may seem strange to us, her presence with her sisters tenderly inspires. Clare never asked a sister to do anything that she was unwilling to do herself. No duty within the San Damiano monastery was beneath her dignity. Her sisters experienced her as humble, kind, and loving. She would wash the feet of her sisters and give them water from her own hands.

Once, on a Thursday during Lent, Clare was washing the feet of a serving sister who had returned to the monastery. When she bent down to kiss her foot, the sister, thinking herself unworthy of such a favor, pulled her leg back and in the process hit Clare in the mouth. Clare persevered in the spirit of our Lord's service to his disciples, and kissed the sole of the sister's foot.

Within the monastery, Clare consistently exhibited a spirit of joy. There were times when the sisters needed correction, but Clare fulfilled this duty without becoming upset or angry. She rejoiced in the Lord, and was never disturbed. While she wholeheartedly participated in the sufferings of Christ's passion, she treated each sister's body and spirit with respect. She never required more of her sisters than they were given to bear by grace. She was able to discern both the bodily and spiritual needs of each sister. Most touchingly, Clare would go through the dormitory at night to make sure that her sisters were covered from the cold.

When sisters became ill, Clare did the most degrading tasks in order to spare her sisters. She washed the commodes of the sick sisters, and cleansed the feet of the serving sisters. She loved her sisters as herself, and was consistently compassionate toward them. When a sister suffered anguish of spirit, trial, or temptation, Clare would see her privately to console her.

While she was interested in the souls of others, Clare shielded herself from the gossip of the world. When she sent out the serving sisters, she helped them focus on God's beauty in creation rather than on petty rumors and the daily news. "Praise God," she told them, "whenever you see beautiful trees, flowers, bushes, creatures, and in the souls of all people."

Another early companion of Clare, Sister Benvenuta of Perugia, remembered that one of Francis's brothers, Brother Stephen, suffered from a mental illness. Francis sent Brother Stephen to Clare for her blessing. Clare allowed him to pray at San Damiano and he left cured. The sisters said that he never returned to the monastery.

Sister Filippa tells a story of a man who took care of the finances at San Damiano. His little boy had a terrible fever and, not knowing what more to do, he brought the child to Clare so that she could bless him. Clare touched the child and he got better. This healing did not happen immediately, but the father reported that the child had recovered. Apparently, children were not permitted to run around regularly in the monastery, but parents did bring sick children to Clare for her blessing.

Often when people think about St. Clare, they picture her with the Blessed Sacrament. This is because once there was a group of Saracens who attacked the Monastery of San Damiano. The sisters were extremely afraid, but Clare assured them: "Do not be afraid, dear sisters, because the enemy cannot hurt us since the Lord is with us. Trust in the Lord Jesus Christ, because he will save us."

Clare then told the sisters that she would offer herself as a hostage, if necessary, so that nothing evil would happen to them. She went to pray and the Saracens left without harming the sisters. Obviously they discovered that there was nothing of value in the poor monastery and thankfully, left the sisters alone. In regard to this same incident, Sister Francesca adds that Clare went to the entrance of the refectory carrying the Blessed Sacrament in a pyx, with the result that the Saracens left the monastery unharmed.

Sister Amata was Clare's niece. She had suffered for over a year from a fever, cough, pain in her side, and an abdomen filled with fluid. Miserable, she begged for Clare's blessing. Amata reported that Clare placed her hands over her and asked God, if it was good for Amata's soul, to cure her. With Clare's prayer, Amata recovered and never again suffered from this affliction.

Sister Amata also tells the delightful story of Sister Cecilia, who had a suffocating cough that erupted as soon as she tried to eat. One Friday, which was a fast day, Clare beckoned Cecilia to eat a little cake. Sister Cecilia tried to eat, although fearful that she would again suffer a coughing fit. After finishing the cake in deference to Clare, Cecilia was cured of her coughing.

Sister Amata further recalled that a young boy from the town of Perugia had cataracts that covered his eyes. His family brought him to San Damiano and Clare blessed the child. Clare then suggested that her mother, Ortolana, who had joined Clare as a sister at San Damiano, should also bless the child. After Ortolana blessed the boy, the child was healed and Clare gave credit for the cure to her mother. Of course, Ortolana claimed that it was Clare's blessing that supplied the healing.

Sister Cristiana told the story of a heavy monastery door that once fell right on top of Clare. Sister Angeluccia saw the accident and screamed loudly, thinking that Clare had been crushed. Since the sisters could not lift the door off of Clare by themselves, the Franciscan brothers were called and they lifted the door to find Clare unharmed. Cristiana said it seemed to everyone that a mantle of protection had been placed over Clare.

Sister Cecilia was impressed by the fact that even when she was very ill, Clare never wished to be idle. When she could not get out of bed, Clare propped herself up so that she could spin cloth. With this cloth, Clare made corporals and cases covered with silk or precious materials. After she had the corporals blessed by the bishop, Clare sent them to every church in the diocese of Assisi.

Sister Cecilia also related an incident where Francis and Clare had a difference of opinion. Francis had sent five women to San Damiano convinced that they had vocations. Clare, who spent time talking with each woman, decided that she would receive four of them, but did not want to accept the fifth because she felt that she would not persevere. Clare was pressured to accept her, but the woman stayed only about six months.

Perhaps the most delightful story in the *Process* is Sister Cecilia's recollection of the monastery cat. Once when Clare was confined to her bed because of illness she needed a towel, but no one was in the dormitory to get it for her. She somehow was able to convince one of the monastery kittens to drag it to her as best it could. As the cat was bringing her the towel, Clare said: "You naughty thing! Why are you dragging the towel on the ground?" The cat, as if it understood Clare, began to roll the towel so that not so much of it would be on the ground. Clare later told this story to her sisters.

After the commission finished listening to the stories at San Damiano, they went to Assisi to record the stories of laypeople who had known Clare. A knight by the name of Lord Ugolino stated that he had left his wife, Lady Guiduzia, many years before and sent her back in disgrace to her father. When he came to the monastery, Clare told Ugolino that she had a vision that he would take Lady Guiduzia back and would have a son with her, and that would give him great consolation. Convinced, he returned to his wife and had a son, who indeed proved to be a great blessing.

Lord Ranieri of Assisi testified that he was a jilted would-be lover of Clare. He said that Clare had a "beautiful face" and that he proposed to her many times. Other nobles did the same, according to Ranieri, but Clare rejected these advances. The situation was finally settled after Clare's hair was cut, deeming her unmarriageable and in the service of Christ.

The last witness was John de Ventura, who had served as the night watchman in Clare's home in Assisi. He reported that although Clare's family lived a lavish lifestyle and spent extravagant sums, Clare would save the food off her own plate and give it to the poor. Lady Bona, Clare's childhood friend, claimed that Clare often asked Bona to deliver this food to the hungry. Apparently Clare had also taken care of the physical needs of Francis before her conversion because Bona claimed that Clare gave her money to take to St. Mary of the Angels so that the brothers could buy food.

Although she said very little, perhaps Sister Lucia of Rome summarized Clare's life best. According to Lucia, Clare tried to please God, and to teach her sisters how to love God. She showed tender compassion for her sisters both in their physical and spiritual needs. In short, Clare loved greatly both God and neighbor.

A Wondrous Ending

During her last days, Clare was filled with a great love of God as she comforted her grieving sisters, and was gentle and tender toward her own soul. In her final illness, Clare softly uttered many things about the Trinity, then addressed her own soul. "Go securely in peace," Clare advised herself, "because you will have a good escort. God who created you has filled you with the Holy Spirit. God has always looked upon you as a mother gazes on the child whom she loves."

There probably is no other saint in the history of Christian spirituality who reverenced the marvel of her own soul as Clare did. Clare knew that the heavens and earth could not contain their Creator, but that God chose to dwell in the faithful soul. Like Mary, Clare cherished the presence of Christ within the wonder of her being.

As she was dying, Clare consoled her sisters. Her most precious gift was the poverty that she had promised the Lord and St. Francis. She had wanted all her life to have her dependence upon the Lord in poverty affirmed in canon law. The popes who reigned in her lifetime, however, were reluctant to do this because they did not want monasteries of women who did not have the financial resources to care for their own needs.

While the papacy concerned itself with financial exigency, Clare wished to love and follow completely the Poor Christ. In doing so, the considerable dowries of young noblewomen were being given to the poor. Clare's acceptance of poverty was, in fact, a true love of both God and neighbor.

Of course, both Clare and the papacy had legitimate concerns. When Pope Innocent IV learned that Clare was gravely ill, he rushed to Assisi to see her. At San Damiano, Innocent heard Clare's confession and was so moved by her humility and holiness that he decided to grant Clare her final request.

The next day, a brother came to the monastery bearing a letter with the papal seal. Clare's desire to live without property or regular income was now guaranteed in law. Even though she was very close to death, Clare took the precious seal to her lips and kissed it. Clare's last words were: "Blessed in the eyes of the Lord is the death of his faithful ones."

Clare died on August 11, 1253. She left her sisters and all of us the gift of a vibrant and joyful Franciscan spirit. She teaches us to love and care deeply for our own souls, to be compassionate and tender toward those we meet in our daily lives, and to love God with every fiber of our being. Nothing, not even the monastery cat, was too small or insignificant for Clare's attention.

As we go about in our world, let us follow Clare's advice to bless God for every tree, every flower, every creature, every neighbor, and, yes, God's very presence within our own souls.

Bibliography

Bartoli, Marco. *Clare of Assisi* (Quincy, Ill.: Franciscan, 1993).

Carney, Margaret. "Francis and Clare: A Critical Examination of the Sources," *Laurentianum* 30 (1987), pp. 25–60.

Fontes Franciscani. Edited by Enrico Menestò and Stefano Brufani (Assisi, Italy: Edizioni Porziuncola, 1995).

Lainati, Chiara Augusta. *Saint Clare of Assisi* (Assisi, Italy: Edizioni Porziuncola, 1994).

Mueller, Joan. *Clare of Assisi: The Letters to Agnes* (Collegeville, Minn.: Liturgical, 2003).

———. *A Companion to Clare of Assisi: Life, Writings, and Spirituality* (Leiden, Netherlands: Brill, 2010).

———. *The Privilege of Poverty: Clare of Assisi, Agnes of Prague, and the Struggle for a Franciscan Rule for Women* (University Park, Pa.: The Pennsylvania State University Press, 2006).